Class 50s on the route
from Waterloo to Exeter

1 A sight to gladden any Class 50 enthusiast's eyes as No D400 (formerly No 50050 *Fearless*), resplendent in the old dark blue livery, climbs the famous 1 in 37 bank between Exeter St Davids and Exeter Central stations with the 06.45 service from St Davids to Waterloo, the first up train of the day. The date is Saturday 25 May 1991. On weekdays at this time the first up service was 06.11.

No D400 was renovated to its original 1960s-style-livery by the staff at Laira depot and it certainly looks a credit to them. Also no small part was played by the readers of *RAIL* magazine who contributed £3,000 towards is restoration. *RS*

Class 50s on the route from Waterloo to Exeter

Roger Siviter ARPS

Silver Link Publishing Ltd

The Waterloo-Exeter line

CONTENTS

Introduction   7
Class 50 numbers, names, Sectors and withdrawal dates   12
Gradient profiles of the route   13

Waterloo to Salisbury   15
Salisbury to Exeter   59

Index   128

ACKNOWLEDGEMENTS

I should like to thank the many people without whose help a project like this would be impossible:

To the photographers who have put their collections at my disposal.
To John Vaughan for much help and advice.
To my wife Christina for typing, maps and help with the layout.
To Howard Johnston, for the information on page 12.
To my publisher who has given me a free hand.
Last but not least, to the professional railwaymen who make it all possible.

BIBLIOGRAPHY

British Railways Past & Present: No 8 Devon David Mitchell (Silver Link Publishing Ltd)
Waterloo-Exeter Heyday Gerald Siviour & Mike Esau (Ian Allan)
Power of the 50s John Vaughan (OPC)
Profile of the Class 50s John Vaughan (OPC)
Fifties in Devon & Cornwall Roger Siviter (Kingfisher/Runpast)

First published in 1992 as 50s TO EXETER
Reprinted 1992
Reprinted in 2001 as CLASS 50s ON THE ROUTE FROM WATERLOO TO EXETER

British Library Cataloguing in Publication Data

Siviter, Roger
50s to Exeter
I. Title
385.0942

ISBN 0 947971 81 5

Silver Link Publishing Ltd
The Trundle
Ringstead Road
Great Addington
Kettering
Northants
NN14 4BW

Tel/Fax: 01536 330588
email: sales@nostalgiacollection.com
Website: www.nostalgiacollection.com

Printed and bound in Great Britain

2 Transition time at Waterloo, 5 June 1967. In the foreground 'West Country' Class 'Pacific' No 34090 *Sir Eustace Missenden, Southern Railway* is on the empty stock of a Bournemouth train, whilst in the background 'Warship' Class diesel No D827 *Kelly* is at rest after bringing in a morning train from Exeter.

Steam working was to finish on the Southern Region within a few weeks of this picture being taken (9 July) although steam had not been in regular use on the Exeter line since 1965. The 'Warship' diesels worked on the Exeter route between 1964 and 1971.

The holiday being advertised by BOAC is worth noting - 16 days in Nassau from £159! *RS*

INTRODUCTION

The Waterloo to Exeter route of the London & South Western Railway (LSWR) was completed to Exeter in 1860. However, the first sections of the route between London and Worting Junction, just to the west of Basingstoke, were completed in stages between 1838 and 1840 and formed part of the London & Southampton Railway. It was not until 1857 that a single line from Worting Junction to Salisbury was completed, thus giving a direct route from the famous cathedral city to the capital. Andover, which is situated roughly half-way between Basingstoke and Salisbury, was reached in 1854.

At first, the LSWR trains used the GWR station at Salisbury Fisherton Street, the GWR having reached Salisbury in 1856 from Westbury and Warminster. In 1859, with the completion of Fisherton tunnel, the LSWR were able to reach their new terminus, which was situated alongside the GWR station. The famous curved approach to the LSWR station was made necessary because the line had to wind round the Great Western station.

In 1856, the Salisbury & Yeovil Railway Company, with the support of the LSWR, started work on the line west of Salisbury, and Yeovil was reached in June 1860. A few weeks later, on 19 July, an extension to Exeter Queen Street was opened. Originally a shorter coastal route from Salisbury via Dorchester, Bridport and Axminster to Exeter had been planned but, because of the excessive curvatures and steep gradients, the inland route was favoured. Finally, in 1862, the 3/4-mile link down the 1 in 37 bank to Exeter St Davids (GWR) was completed, thus giving the LSWR access to the Crediton line and later on to Plymouth and north Cornwall.

This now meant that Exeter had two direct routes to London, that of the LSWR via Salisbury and the GWR via Bristol, which had been opened much earlier, in 1844. Salisbury to Exeter was originally single track, but was doubled in 1870 - how ironic that most of this section is now once again single track!

Thus the scene was set for many years of rivalry between the GWR and the LSWR (from 1922 the Southern Railway), right through until 1963, when the Western Region of British Railways took control of the line west of Salisbury and demoted it to a secondary route, making it mostly single track.

Although the line is now almost exclusively used for passenger traffic, at one time, especially in the '30s, '40s and '50s, a fair amount of freight was carried, including milk traffic from the West Country. Also, until the 1980s stone trains from Meldon Quarry (Okehampton) were to be seen on the route, but around the middle of that decade these were routed east via Westbury. There were also many troop trains using the line, especially in the days of National Service.

During the most prosperous years of the line, particularly before and after the Second World War, there was also of course a huge amount of holiday traffic for the many seaside resorts of east and north Devon and north Cornwall, with summer Saturdays seeing dozens of trains on the route, the most famous of all being the 'Atlantic Coast Express' ('ACE'), which ran in several portions.

However, from the mid-1960s to the early 1980s there was a general decline in traffic, although from around 1983 there has been a steady increase in passenger traffic, and optimism is high for the future of the line.

Over the years a wide variety of steam motive power has been seen on the line, from Drummond T9 4-4-0s of the LSWR, 'Lord Nelson' and 'King Arthur' 4-6-0s of the SR and, post-war, what were arguably the most famous classes of all on the route, Bulleid's 'Merchant Navy' and 'West Country' 'Pacifics'.

From the mid-1960s diesel motive power took over from steam, first with the popular 'Warship' Class of hydraulic diesels, then, in the 1970s, the Class 33s, or 'Cromptons' as they are popularly known. Because the Class 33s were only 1,550 bhp compared to the 2,200 bhp of the 'Warships', there followed an increase in journey times, the average journey being just under 4 hours. This coincided with the lowest ebb of the line's fortunes, although it should be added that the 'Cromptons' were and still are very reliable machines.

3 Steam forerunners of the Class 50s were the 'Merchant Navy' and 'West Country'/'Battle of Britain' 'Pacifics'. In this historic scene, photographed on 21 August 1958, unrebuilt 'Merchant Navy' 'Pacific' No 35003 *Royal Mail* is seen at speed between Semley and Gillingham with the first portion (from Padstow) of the up 'Atlantic Coast Express', the crack train on the route, commonly known as the 'ACE'. On summer Saturdays in the 1950s many portions of this train were run to serve the seaside resorts of east and north Devon and north Cornwall.

The 'Merchant Navy' 'Pacifics', designed by Bulleid, were first introduced on the Southern Railway in 1941. The class were all rebuilt by the late 1950s with Walschaerts valve gear and modified details, as well as the removal of the air-smoothed casing. *Hugh Ballantyne*

4 'West Country' 'light Pacific' No 34013 *Okehampton* departs from Salisbury with the 3.05 pm local train to Exeter on 18 April 1964. In the background M7 0-4-4 tank No 30025 is seen shunting vans. The 'West Country' 'Pacifics', as well as being used on the local services on the line, were also used on the through expresses, especially on summer Saturdays. Unlike the larger 'Merchant Navy' 'Pacifics', not all of the class were rebuilt, and so retained their streamlined casing until they were scrapped at the end of steam. Happily, examples of both 'Merchant Navy' and 'West Country' (unrebuilt and rebuilt) locomotives have been preserved and can be seen today on the main line, as well as on the many preserved lines throughout the country. *Hugh Ballantyne*

In 1980 the first Class 50 locomotives appeared on the line and this coincided with the start of its reviving fortunes, brought about by local management. The English Electric Class 50 locomotives were built in 1967-8; originally leased to BR by their builders, they were subsequently owned by BR. These powerful 16-cylinder machines had 2,700 bhp and a maximum tractive effort of 48,500 lbs, with a top speed of 100 mph.

The Class 50s, or 'Hoovers' as they are popularly known, first worked on the London Midland Region of BR, mainly on the West Coast route. During electrification of this route in the early 1970s they were used mainly in pairs between Crewe and Glasgow. From 1974 they were gradually transferred to the Western Region, this transfer being completed by 1976.

Around this time their numbers were changed to the 50000 series (see page 12), having originally been numbered D400 onwards. It was during 1978 that the class was named after warships.

During the late 1970s locomotive No 50006 was completely refurbished by Doncaster Works to obtain greater availability, and the rest of the class had followed suit by the early 1980s, most of them also being turned out in the new BR livery ('large logo') in which, in the author's humble opinion, they looked at their finest.

At first their job was to replace the Class 52 locomotives ('Westerns') on the Paddington-West of England services and on the Paddington-Birmingham route, but the advent of the Inter-City 125 High Speed Trains (HSTs) on the West of England services in 1979-80 meant that some of the Class 50 locomotives became available for the Waterloo-Exeter route. Driver training commenced in the latter months of 1979 with one train each way per day. Thus from 1980 onwards the Class 50s became the predominant motive power on the route, right up to the present day when they are to be replaced by Express Sprinter units.

The Class 50s' power and speed led to considerable accelerations of the services, the average journey time becoming around $3^1/_2$ hours; also of course increased loading was possible, if necessary. Stations were reopened and in 1986 a loop was added at Tisbury large enough to accommodate a 12-coach train, thus helping to increase punctuality.

As the years have gone by, certain classes of diesel locomotives have become very popular with enthusiasts, notably the 'Western' hydraulics and the famous 'Deltics' of the Eastern Region. It would be fair to say that the Class 50s are now also in that elite category. There is a Class 50 Society, and plans are afoot for the preservation of several of the class. Also of interest is that during the last decade Class 50s have been turned out in many different liveries, from the original livery and numbering through to that of Network SouthEast.

All of which brings us to the purpose of this book, which is to show a journey from Waterloo to Exeter behind these powerful machines, surely worthy modern traction successors to the steam locomotives of old. Anyone who has ridden behind these fine diesel locomotives will remember the stirring sounds they made as they literally roared up a steep gradient, a sound never to be forgotten.

5 The steam era finished on the route in the mid-1960s, and from 1964 until 1971 the Type 4 'Warship' Class diesels were the principal locomotives used on the Waterloo-Exeter services. In this view, taken on 2 July 1967, No D826 *Jupiter* is seen at speed near Basing on the old SR four-track section with a mid-morning Waterloo-Exeter train. Typical of the times, there is a very mixed rake of coaching stock, including some in 'Southern green'.

The first 'Warships' were built by BR in 1958 (Nos D800-D832, D866-D870) and had two Bristol Siddeley-Maybach engines. The second batch (D833-D865) was introduced in 1960 and was built by North British using their own engines. Both types of locomotives had hydraulic transmission. *RS*

6 Whereas the 'Warships' were the principal diesel traction of the 1960s (with only the occasional appearances by other types such as the 'Westerns' and 'Hymeks'), in the 1970s the Class 33s held sway. These Type 3 locomotives, introduced in 1960 and built by the Birmingham Railway Carriage and Wagon Company, had electric transmission and four Crompton Parkinson motors, hence the popular nickname 'Cromptons'. Because of their lower bhp (1,150 compared to the 2,000-2,400 of the 'Warships'), journey times were increased and no acceleration took place until the advent of the Class 50s in 1980. Nevertheless, they were and still are reliable machines and can still be seen on the line today on filling-in turns.

This scene, on 29 August 1970, shows Class 33 No D6517 (renumbered No 33105) passing Gillingham at speed with the 08.00 Waterloo-Exeter service. By now parts of the line had been singled and the train is running through on the old up line. *Hugh Ballantyne*

Class 50 numbers, names, Sectors and withdrawal dates

Loco	Final sector		Withdrawn	Loco	Final sector		Withdrawn
50001 *Dreadnought*	NWXA		19.04.91	50032 *Courageous*	DCWA		15.10.90
50002 *Superb*	NWXA	Preserved	15.07.91	50033 *Glorious*	NWXA	BR Railtour loco	*
50003 *Temeraire*	NWXA		09.09.91	50034 *Furious*	DCW		29.06.90
50004 *St Vincent*	DCWA		22.06.90	50035 *Ark Royal*	INWXC	Preserved	03.08.90
50005 *Collingwood*	NWXA		11.12.90	50036 *Victorious*	NWXA		19.04.91
50006 *Neptune*	–		20.07.87	50037 *Illustrious*	NWXA		09.09.91
50007 *Sir Edward Elgar*				50038 *Formidable*	NXXA		27.09.88
(formerly *Hercules*)	NWXA	BR Railtour loco	**15.07.91	50039 *Implacable*	NWRA		04.06.89
50008 *Thunderer*	CEJC	BR Reserve loco	*	50040 *Leviathan*			
50009 *Conqueror*	NWXC		11.01.91	(later *Centurion*)	DCWA		03.08.90
50010 *Monarch*	NXXA		27.09.88	50041 *Bulwark*	NSSA		17.04.90
50011 *Centurion*	–		24.02.87	50042 *Triumph*	DCWA	Preserved	15.10.90
50012 *Benbow*	DCWA		16.01.89	50043 *Eagle*	NWXA	Preserved	01.02.90
50013 *Agincourt*	NXXA		31.03.88	50044 *Exeter*	NWXA	Preserved	11.01.91
50014 *Warspite*	–		14.12.87	50045 *Achilles*	NWXC		11.12.90
50015 *Valiant*	CEJC	BR Reserve loco	*	50046 *Ajax*	NWXA		25.03.92
50016 *Barham*	NWRA		10.07.90	50047 *Swiftsure*	PXXA		13.04.88
50017 *Royal Oak*	NWXA	Preserved	09.09.91	50048 *Dauntless*	NWXA		15.07.91
50018 *Resolution*	NWXA		22.07.91	50049 *Defiance*	NWXA	Preserved	16.08.91
50019 *Ramillies*	DCWA	Preserved	19.09.90	50050 *Fearless*			
50020 *Revenge*	DCWA		27.07.90	(now D400)	NWXA	BR Railtour loco	*
50021 *Rodney*	DCWA	Preserved	17.04.90				
50022 *Anson*	RXXA		20.09.88	* Still in stock 1 May 1992		** Reinstated 27 March 1992	
50023 *Howe*	DCWA		15.10.90	Pool codes:			
50024 *Vanguard*	NWXA		01.02.90	CEJC (Central Services Civil Link, Engineers)			
50025 *Invincible*	NWRA		14.08.89	NXXA (Network SE General Pool)			
50026 *Indomitable*	NWXA		11.12.90	PXXA (Provincial General Pool)			
50027 *Lion*	NWXA	Preserved	23.07.91	NSSA (Network SE Solent & Sarum)			
50028 *Tiger*	NWXA		01.02.90	FTLL (Chemicals, Laira)			
50029 *Renown*	NWXA	Retained for spares	25.03.92	NWRA (Network SE Western Region)			
50030 *Repulse*	NWXA	Retained for spares	*	NWRC (Network SE Western Region Reserve)			
50031 *Hood*	NWXA	Preserved	05.08.91	DCWA (Regional Civil Engineer, Western Region)			

Class 50 operation on the Waterloo-Exeter route was due to end in May 1992, but the run-down of the class can be traced back to April 1987, with the end of major overhauls at Doncaster. The first withdrawal from service was No 50011 *Centurion*, taken to Crewe to act as a static testbed for repaired power units; these were then transported to Laira, which took over the major repair responsibility. Even if *Centurion's* demise was seen as meeting an exceptional need, the withdrawal of a second loco, No 50006 *Neptune*, in July was not. An acute shortage of spares, plus punitive cash limits on repairs, was a portent for the future.

The full effect of Sectorisation was felt from May 1989, when the 50-strong fleet was carved up into four distinct groups: NSE (Waterloo-Exeter and Thames & Chiltern routes); the Regional Civil Engineer; and Railfreight. Thus it was that you could expect to perm any one from 13 for services out of Waterloo (Nos 50001/2/3/17/8/9/27/8/9/41/3/4/8), 16 out of Paddington (Nos 50023/4/5/6/30/1/2/3/4/5/6/7/9/40/6/50), 12 on engineer's trains (Nos 50004/5/7/8/9/12/5/6/20/1/42/5), and a solitary example on china clay workings in Cornwall, the experimental No 50149.

The Class 50s' sphere of operation shrank. The Paddington services had gone over to Class 47/4 operation by August 1990, and the engineering locos, often in poor condition, had either been scrapped or transferred as top-ups for the Waterloo-Exeter route by the late autumn of the same year. However, the release of redundant Edinburgh-Glasgow push-pull Class 47/7s was not the immediate solution that NSE had hoped for. Many 50s had been condemned with faults as minor as a defective turbocharger or tyre flats, but the brakes were slammed on the rapid run-down and the three survivors, Nos 50029/30/3, were allowed to operate until they collapsed with mechanical exhaustion.

Preservation groups from Crewe to Cornwall had saved no fewer than 11 examples by the end of 1991, and readers of *RAIL* magazine clubbed together for the repainting of No 50050 back to its original 1968 blue livery as No D400. BR responded by returning it to main-line running, and added Nos 50007/33 to the prestige fleet.

Information by courtesy of Howard Johnston

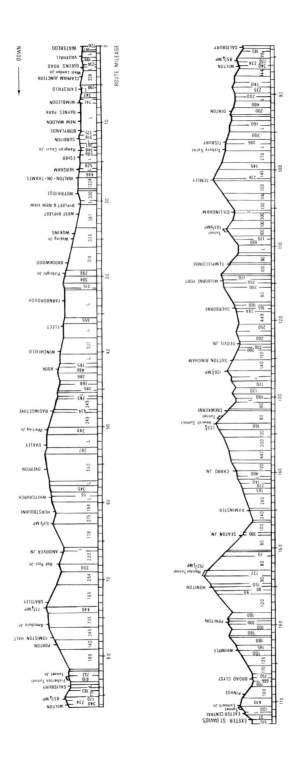

Gradient profile, Waterloo–Exeter

7 Although this book covers the main LSWR route from Waterloo to Exeter, I have included this picture to show the main diversionary route between Basingstoke and Salisbury, which follows the LSWR route from Worting Junction via Eastleigh, St Denys, Southampton and Romsey to Tunnel Junction, Salisbury. This is not only a diversionary route for engineering work, etc, but is also used by the Plymouth-Exeter-Southampton-Waterloo trains on summer Saturdays, as well as the service from Plymouth to Brighton (via Portsmouth).

This wintry scene taken on 16 March 1985 (which proves that it does snow in the south of England!) shows Class 50 No 50013 *Agincourt* approaching St Denys station with the 10.35 Waterloo-Exeter service, diverted because of engineering work near Andover. On the right is the line from Southampton to Portsmouth. *Michael J.Collins*

WATERLOO TO SALISBURY

The route was originally operated by the London & South Western Railway, but was then grouped under the Southern Railway whose style endures in the then ultra-modern station furniture built of ferro-concrete. Four-track lines, two with third-rail electric supply, leave Waterloo in a generally south-westerly direction, curving with the River Thames across which can be seen Big Ben. After Lambeth and Vauxhall, we pass through Nine Elms, now home to the New Covent Garden market, then under the lines for Brixton and Victoria, and through the tangle of lines at Clapham Junction station.

The next 6 miles are fairly level, running through Earlsfield, Wimbledon, Raynes Park and New Malden (formerly Malden) stations, after which a line branches north for Twickenham. We cross Hogsmill River into Berrylands station, then run through a long cutting to Surbiton and, crossing the border into Surrey, we reach Hampton Court Junction. At Esher, the station lies between the golf course and the race course at Sandown Park. To the north as we cross the River Mole gleam a chain of reservoirs. After Hersham and Walton-on-Thames, a mile-long cutting takes us to Weybridge station. Between this and the next station, Byfleet & New Haw (formerly West Weybridge), is a triangular junction, the west chord for goods, and the huge Brooklands works lies to the south.

We leave the Thames valley and climb gently following the Basingstoke canal, passing West Byfleet station (formerly Byfleet) to Woking, with its junction for Guildford. The landscape now changes from London suburbia to sandy birchwoods. At Brookwood the line runs between an enormous cemetery and the military camps of Bisley and Pirbright, then rises for 3 miles beside a flight of canal locks. Half-way up a line branches for Aldershot, after which is the mile-long Deepcut. The line emerges to cross two lines flanking Broadwater valley and the Hampshire border.

After Farnborough, the next station, the line runs nearly due west in a dead straight line for 15 miles to Basingstoke. Skirting the famous airfield, we then run over Fleet Pond on a causeway to Fleet station. The M3 with its much-appreciated service station lies just north of here, and the motorway crosses the line between the next two stations of Winchfield and Hook, over a deep cutting, and finally severs the canal at Old Basing, where the line is flanked by an avenue of Lawson cypresses.

Basingstoke is heralded by the great office tower of the AA headquarters. We pass Barton Mill sidings and the junction for Reading on the right. The handsome station is overlooked by church ruins and cherry trees. Two miles further west we pass under Battledown flyover at Worting Junction, where the electrified line leaves us for Southampton, the original L&SR route. Our two tracks take us through Oakley station, then over its summit. There follows a descent of about 15 miles as far as Andover.

After Overton station we reach Whitchurch, where the landscape changes into white chalk downs. A red-brick viaduct carries us high above watercress farms to Hurstbourne, where there used to be a junction station, then we take a mile-long deep cutting through

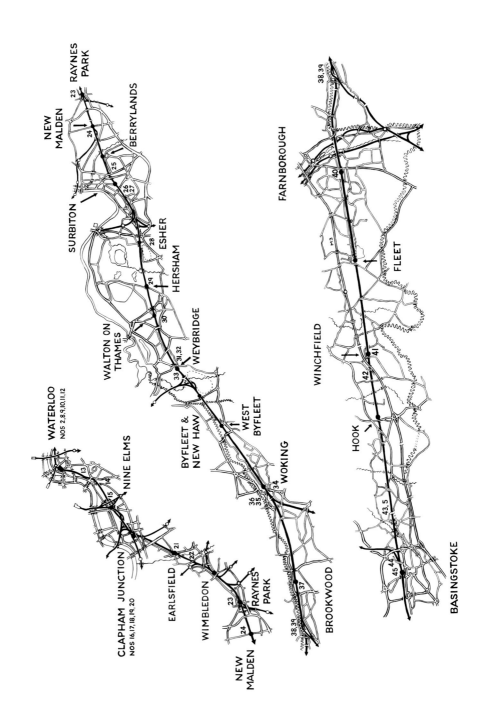

RAYNES PARK
NEW MALDEN
BERRYLANDS
SURBITON
ESHER
HERSHAM
WALTON ON THAMES
WEYBRIDGE
BYFLEET & NEW HAW
WEST BYFLEET
WOKING
WATERLOO NOS 2,8,9,10,11,12
NINE ELMS
CLAPHAM JUNCTION NOS 16,17,18,19,20
EARLSFIELD
WIMBLEDON
RAYNES PARK
NEW MALDEN
BROOKWOOD

FARNBOROUGH
FLEET
WINCHFIELD
HOOK
BASINGSTOKE

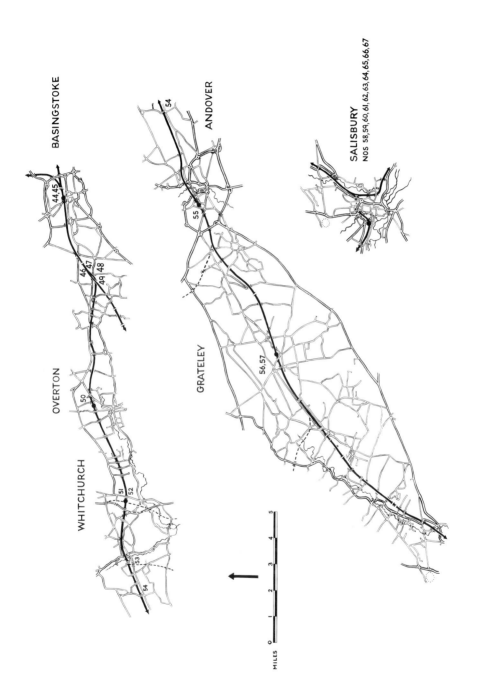

BASINGSTOKE

44,45

46
47
48
49 48

OVERTON

50

WHITCHURCH

51
52

53

54

ANDOVER

54

55

GRATELEY

56,57

SALISBURY
NOS 58,59,60,61,62,63,64,65,66,67

MILES
0 1 2 3 4 5

The route: Waterloo to Salisbury (numbers refer to plates)

8 Our journey to the West Country starts at Waterloo station on 27 April 1991, but in reverse! Class 50 No 50048
Dauntless is seen at the buffer stops at platform 13 having just arrived with the 06.45 train from Exeter.

    Compare this scene to plate 2 (page 6) which was taken some 24 years earlier and, as can be seen, many changes
have taken place, notably to the platform entrance area, modern partitions having replaced the ornate railings of earlier days.

    This fine old station, situated on the southern side of the River Thames just south-east of the Palace of
Westminster, dates back to around 1840. The first main route ran to Basingstoke and Southampton (the London &
Southampton Railway). Salisbury was reached in 1857 and Exeter in 1860 by the then London & South Western
Railway (LSWR), the forerunner of the Southern Railway. *RS*

the chalk of Devil's Dyke, hung with yews and wayfaring trees.

    Andover station has much dismantled trackbed, but one bay has been attractively
landscaped, and the subway is brightly tiled. The line now rises for 5 miles past the airfield and the branch for Ludgershall Camp to Grateley station. From Amesbury Junction,
just beyond, a spur used to run off to the right for Bulford Camp, of which the author has
vivid memories of his National Service! We now cross the Wiltshire border and run
4 miles south-west in a dead straight line following The Portway, a Roman road, and get
our first sight of Salisbury's famous cathedral.

    There is a notoriously sharp right curve just before Tunnel Junction and Fisherton tun-
nel. Our line originally terminated straight ahead at Milford (1858), but after the curve
was built to join the GWR line from Southampton, this surplus end of track was disman-
tled, but has recently been reinstated to form a triangle. Finally we run through Fisherton
Tunnel and down a sweeping curve past an old water tower into Salisbury station.

9 In latter years, Exeter-line trains generally operated out of platforms 12 and 13 at Waterloo, the platforms being used alternately. No 50007 *Sir Edward Elgar*, resplendent in 'BR green' and complete with GWR-style name and number plates, waits to leave platform 13 with the 11.15 train to Exeter on 27 April 1991.

Sir Edward Elgar was the name of Great Western Railway 'Castle' Class 4-6-0 steam locomotive No 7005, which was built in 1946 and withdrawn in 1964. As with No 50007, which was formerly named *Hercules*, No 7005 was first named *Lamphey Castle*, but the name was changed in 1957. *RS*

10 Class 50 No 50048 (see plate 8) has now 'missed a turn' and is ready to leave platform 12 with the next train to Exeter, the 13.15 service calling at Woking, Basingstoke, Andover, Salisbury and then most stations to Exeter St Davids. The Waterloo-Salisbury service, which was Class 50-hauled until withdrawals in the latter years, stops at principal stations between the two cities. *RS*

11 and 12   The next two pictures, taken on 28 April 1989, were photographed from the block of flats situated just west of the station, an excellent location from which to view the comings and goings at Waterloo. In the upper view we see No 50043 *Eagle* bathed in spring sunshine as it heads south out of Waterloo with the 17.34 service to Yeovil Junction. Within a mile or so the line makes a turn to the south-west, the direction it more or less follows until Exeter. The clear lighting picks out the contrast between the old and new architecture of inner London.

In the lower scene, No 50041 *Bulwark* approaches Waterloo with the 15.08 service from Salisbury. In the background are the crowded streets of the ancient borough of Lambeth, whilst in the foreground are the Waterloo arches, some of which are still used for small businesses. *Both Gavin Morrison*

13 With Big Ben and the Palace of Westminster in the background, No 50027 *Lion* looks a fine sight as it approaches Vauxhall with the 09.15 Waterloo-Salisbury service on 19 August 1989. The line follows the course of the River Thames until it reaches Clapham Junction, some 4 miles from Waterloo. *Gavin Morrison*

14 On a cold November day in 1987, No 50015 *Valiant*, in charge of the 13.10 Waterloo-Exeter, makes steady progress on the gently curving track between Vauxhall and Queen's Road, Battersea. This area, known as Nine Elms, was once famous for its locomotive shed - No 70A. The steam motive power depot was located to the right-hand side of the picture and was the last steam shed in inner London, steam traction having lasted until 9 July 1967 with the completion of the Bournemouth line's electrification. The area where the shed was located is now a fruit market, which has replaced Covent Garden market. *Michael J.Collins*

15 Turning round from the previous picture, we see No 50039 *Implacable* heading through Nine Elms with a morning Exeter-Waterloo express in February 1989. The coaching stock is a mixture of the old BR livery (blue and white) and the new red, white and blue of Network SouthEast. The locomotive is still in the older livery in which most of this class was painted in the early 1980s when the locomotives were refurbished at Doncaster Works. *Michael J.Collins*

16 Some 4 miles out of Waterloo is situated what is arguably the most famous railway junction in the world, and certainly the busiest - Clapham. Viewed from the station overbridge with the London skyline in the distance, an unidentified Class 50 approaches the station with the 19.10 Waterloo-Exeter train on 18 May 1982. *John Vaughan*

17 On Saturday 27 April 1991 No 50048 *Dauntless* speeds through Clapham Junction with the 13.15 Waterloo-Exeter service. Dominating the scene is the famous signal box. *RS*

18 A view looking to the south-west at Clapham Junction (taken from the box). In the foreground are the lines to Windsor and Reading, while on the left-hand side are the suburban lines for south-east London and Oxted, and the main line from Victoria to Gatwick Airport, the route of the famous Gatwick Express, which runs at 15-minute intervals every day. On 12 August 1989 Class 50 No 50044 *Exeter* heads for Waterloo with the 14.17 service from its namesake city. *Gavin Morrison*

19 On the morning of 7 May 1990 No 50045 *Achilles* pulls away from Clapham Junction and heads west with the 09.15 Waterloo-Exeter train. The first stop for this train will be Woking, Surrey, a distance of just over 24 miles from Waterloo, and the time allowed is 25 minutes. This necessitates some smart running to maintain a near 60 mph start-to-stop schedule.

In a few hundred yards the lines in the left-hand foreground will swing away to the south-east for the Gatwick and Oxted routes. *Gavin Morrison*

20 On 7 May 1990 No 50028 *Tiger* leaves Clapham cutting and approaches Clapham Junction with the 06.45 service from Exeter, due to arrive at the capital at 10.13. For passengers requiring an earlier arrival at Waterloo, the timetable of that period provided an 05.56 departure from Exeter St Davids, arriving at Waterloo at 09.16, thus ensuring a full day's business. This earlier train would also make it possible to commute to London on a daily basis from the West Country - I wonder if any hardy soul has attempted it! *Gavin Morrison*

21 In pleasant scenery near Earlsfield (between Clapham and Wimbledon) No 50044 *Exeter* looks to be making brisk progress with the 11.10 Waterloo-Exeter service on 16 July 1988. Looking at this scene it is difficult to imagine that the train is still only around 5 miles from Waterloo. *Gavin Morrison*

22   With a London Transport train in the background, and the up slow line flyover on the left, Class 50 No 50027 *Lion* approaches Railway Staff Halt at Wimbledon with the 12.20 Exeter-Waterloo service on 13 May 1989. This location is approximately 1 mile north-east of Wimbledon station and the halt is for the use of railway personnel only, not being advertised in the public timetable. *John Vaughan*

23   A mile or so west of Wimbledon is Raynes Park, the junction for Epsom and Dorking, and subsequently the Brighton to Portsmouth line via Horsham and Arundel Junction. Also at Motspur Park Junction, 2 miles south of Raynes Park on the line to Epsom, is the line to Chessington, famous for its zoo and miniature railway.

At Raynes Park on 13 May 1989, in original Network SouthEast livery but with unusual black window surrounds, is No 50023 *Howe* with the 11.10 from Waterloo to Exeter. The Epsom-Chessington line diverges on the right. Note also the signal box on the right-hand side. *John Vaughan*

24   Class 50 No 50025 *Invincible* was to suffer an ignominious end in a crash at West Ealing. However, it was a different story at the start of the new summer timetable for 1980 when, on 12 May, it was photographed pulling through New Malden in lovely spring sunshine with the 06.26 service from Exeter to Waterloo.

1980 was the first year that this powerful class of English Electric diesels was in regular use on the line, replacing the less powerful but nonetheless reliable Class 33s or 'Cromptons'. This unrefurbished locomotive is in the original BR blue livery. After refurbishment most of the locomotives were turned out in the 'large logo' livery. *John Vaughan*

25 By now our journey has taken us well into commuter-land. This scene, taken at Surbiton in the heart of Surrey, shows No 50002 *Superb* racing away from the Southern Railway station with the 09.40 from Exeter to Waterloo, on 16 July 1988.

When this modern station was opened in the 1930s, it was hailed as the ultimate in suburban station architecture, and many photographs of it (particularly of the frontage) appeared in the railway press of the day, as well as in the Southern Railway's own publicity outlets. What made it different was that it was constructed in ferro-concrete instead of more traditional brick. *Gavin Morrison*

26 On 3 November 1984 No 50012 *Benbow* approaches Surbiton station with the 05.48 train from Exeter St Davids to Waterloo. This train, which was timed to reach Waterloo at 09.15 - taking 207 minutes to do the 172$^1/_2$ miles, an average of around 50 mph - was the first up service of the day from Exeter. Travellers from Gillingham, with a 05.45 train, and from Salisbury, with 06.14, 06.40 and 07.15 departures, were given the option of an earlier arrival at Waterloo. *Michael J. Collins*

27 With a full load of nine bogies, No 50040 *Leviathan* raises the echoes in Surbiton as it blasts westwards with the 13.10 Waterloo-Exeter train on 6 August 1984. *John Vaughan*

28 Framed in Esher's down signal gantry and bedecked with miniature snowploughs (one of the few members of the class to carry them) is No 50018 *Resolution* speeding the 09.50 Salisbury-Waterloo service towards the capital on 12 January 1991. A Portsmouth-bound 'Greyhound' unit disappears westward. The main route for Guildford and Portsmouth branches south just west of Woking, but between Surbiton and Esher is the junction for the suburban route to Guildford via Oxshott. Esher is also the station for Sandown Park racecourse, situated within walking distance of the station. *John Vaughan*

29 On a sunny winter's day, 12 January 1991, the 11.18 Salisbury-Waterloo train with No 50033 *Glorious* in charge passes through Hersham station. With only six coaches in tow, this would seem to be a very easy task for this powerful locomotive, with its 16 cylinders and 2,700 bhp. Worthy of note are the wooden platforms. *John Vaughan*

30 No 50018 *Resolution* (in original blue livery) heads for London on the up fast line at Walton on Thames on 10 September 1981 with the 06.26 train from Exeter. *John Vaughan*

31 Weybridge station is situated at the end of a deep cutting which starts about a mile and a half to the east of the station, and this first scene, taken on 6 August 1988, well illustrates this. The train is the 06.42 Exeter-Waterloo service, hauled by No 50027 *Lion*. In the left-hand background is the junction for the line to Chertsey and Staines. *Gavin Morrison*

32 The elegant two-arch road bridge that straddles the eastern end of Weybridge station dominates the scene as No 50031 *Hood* speeds through the station with the 18.15 Waterloo-Salisbury on 27 April 1991. *Hood* was one of the last locomotives carrying the 'large logo' livery still in service at this date, and in fact was beautifully repainted by Plymouth Laira depot within a few weeks of this picture being taken (see plate 132). Some idea of the depth of the cutting at Weybridge can be gained from this picture. *RS*

33 On the same day as the previous picture, No 50049 *Defiance* approaches Weybridge station from the west with the 14.22 Exeter-Waterloo train. For around 18 months of its life, from autumn 1987 until early 1989, this locomotive was renumbered No 50149, painted in Rail Freight grey livery, and modified for Rail Freight service. The main modification required was the use of re-geared bogies, similar to those used on the Class 37s. The idea was to obtain more work out of the class as the need for them on passenger trains declined. In the event, this locomotive was the only one to be modified; as stated before, it was returned to NSE livery and to normal specification early in 1989. *RS*

34 Looking smart in the old blue livery, No 50018 *Resolution* pulls away from the Woking stop with the 11.10 Waterloo-Exeter train on 15 May 1982. Note the absence of the front headlight, which denotes that this locomotive had yet to be refurbished at Doncaster Works. Class 73 electro-diesel locomotive No 73129 is stabled on the left-hand side of the picture.

Woking station still boasts wooden platform canopies, as well as a 'modern' Southern Railway concrete signal box. *Michael J. Collins*

35 Pulling through the busy-looking goods yard to the west of Woking station is No 50013 *Agincourt* with the 11.10 Waterloo-Exeter service on 9 March 1985. This locomotive was an early casualty of the class, being withdrawn in 1988. On the right-hand side of the picture is the junction for the line to Guildford and Portsmouth. *Gavin Morrison*

36 No 50037 *Illustrious* catches the last rays of the winter sun as it nears Woking with the 12.25 Exeter-Waterloo service on 12 January 1991. *John Vaughan*

37 After leaving Woking, the old LSWR line to the west is four-track as far as Worting Junction, where the Exeter and Bournemouth lines split. Speeding through Brookwood station on the up main line is No D400 in charge of the Saturdays-only 10.45 Plymouth-Waterloo via Southampton service on 27 April 1991. The line to Southampton branches off at Tunnel Junction, Salisbury, and regains the Exeter-Waterloo line at Worting Junction. The large cemetery at Brookwood is situated just to the south of the station, and a spur used to run from the station to the chapel for Londoners' funeral trains. RS

38 Shortly beyond Brookwood is the junction for Aldershot, which is situated near the 'Guards' depot at Pirbright Camp. No 50017 *Royal Oak* with the 13.15 Waterloo-Exeter train was photographed just to the west of Pirbright Junction on 20 April 1991. This lovely wooded area is on the Surrey-Hampshire borders. RS

39 Turning round from the previous picture, we see No 50031 *Hood* in charge of the 12.25 Exeter-Waterloo service on 27 April 1991. In the background is the Basingstoke Canal which the line follows for 10 miles from the outskirts of Weybridge. *RS*

40 Farnborough, the home of the world-famous air show, is our next location. Although the station clock is out of order, there is nothing wrong with No 50029 *Renown* as it speeds through with the 15.10 Waterloo-Exeter service on 19 July 1986. For the most part, the route from Waterloo to Exeter is undulating; however, the line around Farnborough is level for several miles. *John Vaughan*

41 On 26 July 1991 No 50046 Ajax (the last Class 50 in service with the 'large logo' livery) hurries through the attractive station of Winchfield with the 11.00 Waterloo-Exeter train. Looking at the number of cars in the station car park, it seems as though this area, some 40 miles from Waterloo, is ideal for commuting to the capital.

Note the contrast in the station canopies, the older rounded design on the left and the newer angular version on the right. Winchfield, as with many stations on this route (and indeed throughout the country), once boasted a small goods yard where the daily pick-up goods would call. RS

42   After leaving Winchfield the line runs through a deep cutting, passing under the M3 motorway. In this scene, taken on 26 September 1987, the 09.10 Waterloo-Exeter train hauled by No 50017 *Royal Oak* is just leaving the cutting between Winchfield and Hook. From here the line runs through pastureland until the outskirts of Basingstoke are reached, some 6 miles away. *Michael J. Collins*

43   On a glorious spring day, 20 April 1991, No 50048 *Dauntless* speeds through Basing on the up main with the 11.20 Exeter-Waterloo service. *RS*

44 No 50027 *Lion* with the 13.15 Waterloo-Exeter train passes the modern signal box situated at the eastern end of Basingstoke station at the junction of the London and Reading lines.

   The line to Reading is part of a very important cross-country route being used by trains from the North of England to the South Coast, which run via Oxford and Birmingham New Street. These trains, together with the Exeter line services, Bournemouth trains, local trains and freight services, make Basingstoke a very busy junction. *RS*

45 Basingstoke station boasts four through platforms still with Southern Railway-style canopies and palm trees!

   No 50037 *Illustrious* pulls into platform 2 on 11 April 1991 with the 11.15 Waterloo-Exeter service, having taken 47 minutes for the 47³/₄ miles from Waterloo, including a stop at Woking - an average speed of well over 60 mph. *RS*

46 Looking a bit grubby and a little tired but going like a 'good 'un', No 50008 *Thunderer* blasts past the terraced houses at Worting Junction with the 08.10 Waterloo-Exeter train on 2 July 1988. Worting, situated 2 miles west of Basingstoke station, is where the Exeter and the Southampton/Bournemouth lines part company via the famous Battledown flyover. *John Vaughan*

47 On 12 August 1991 No 50002 *Superb* pulls away from Worting Junction with the 11.00 Waterloo-Exeter service. The train is on the down Salisbury line which, in a few hundred yards, swings westwards under Battledown flyover. The down Bournemouth line is the near line. The up line from Southampton and Bournemouth is the upper level track on the left-hand side of the picture, which rejoins the other routes at Worting Junction. *RS*

48 No 50004 *St Vincent* winds the 08.17 Exeter St Davids to Waterloo around the curve beneath Battledown fly-over near Worting Junction on 26 September 1987. The original layout at Worting was on one level, but was altered at the end of the last century (1897), when the flyover carrying the up Bournemouth line was constructed. *John Vaughan*

49 Providing music to the ears of enthusiasts is, appropriately, No 50007 *Sir Edward Elgar* (resplendent in green livery) as it hurries away under Battledown flyover with the 10.15 Waterloo-Salisbury service on 20 April 1991. The down Bournemouth line is clearly visible in the foreground. *RS*

50 No 50017 *Royal Oak* passes through Overton station with the 08.17 Exeter-Waterloo train on 25 November 1988. Overton is some 5 miles from Worting Junction, from which point the Exeter line is double track through to Salisbury. From Salisbury to Exeter, with exceptions, the line has been singled, but in 1986 a loop was put in just to the east of Tisbury station, which has helped punctuality. *John Vaughan*

51 Approaching Whitchurch on 11 April 1991 is No 50048 *Dauntless* with the 09.15 ECS (empty coaching stock) working from Waterloo to Eastleigh. After a short stay at Eastleigh, the same locomotive will take the empty stock to Salisbury, which will then form the 15.13 Salisbury to Waterloo service. *RS*

52 Whitchurch still boasts a fine-looking station, complete with LSWR station buildings and splendid platform canopies. No 50046 *Ajax* accelerates through the station and heads for Waterloo with the 08.11 service from Exeter on 11 April 1991.

In the background can be seen the A34 trunk road, linking the Midlands with Southampton via Newbury. Also, just west of the station, the ex-GWR route from Newbury to Winchester (and Southampton) ran under the line. This route, known originally as the Didcot, Newbury & Southampton Railway (DN&S) provided a north-to-south connection for the GWR, but was closed in the early 1960s. *RS*

53 Some 2 miles to the west of Whitchurch lies Hurstbourne viaduct, one of the few viaducts on the line. It crosses the River Bourne (which runs into the River Test) and over the watercress beds for which the area is famous.
     In May 1987 No 50007 *Sir Edward Elgar* crosses the eight-arch viaduct with a morning Exeter to Waterloo train. Just to the west of the viaduct was Hurstbourne station (closed in 1964) which was the junction for the line to Fullerton on the Andover Junction to Eastleigh line. *Michael J. Collins*

54 After leaving Hurstbourne viaduct the line climbs at 1 in 275 through a deep and lengthy chalk cutting. The early evening sun highlights the cutting and No 50033 *Glorious* as it heads westwards for Andover with the 15.15 Waterloo-Exeter train on 12 August 1991. As just mentioned, this area is ideal for the growing of watercress, mainly because the springs bubbling through the chalk strata are so pure and reliable.
     Hurstbourne station and junction were situated just before the start of the cutting. *RS*

55 No 50017 *Royal Oak* accelerates away from Andover on 1 September 1990 with the 14.15 Waterloo-Salisbury train. A long lens accentuates the gradient (1 in 220) which trains face in the westbound direction. The fine LSWR station has been restored with the help of the local authority and the TSB Trust Co and is an indication of the revival of the line.
     Andover is the junction for the freight-only line to Ludgershall, which in the late 1980s played host to a number of steam specials. This secondary route originally ran through to Savernake, and there was also a short branch line from Ludgershall to the military town of Tidworth.
     The large building in the left-hand background is owned by UK Fertilizers. *RS*

56 and 57 Two views at Grateley taken ten years apart, which show well the reviving fortunes of this West Country main line.

In the first picture, taken on 12 July 1980, No 50019 *Ramillies* pulls away from Grateley's weed-covered platforms with the 06.50 service from Waterloo to Exeter. At the time this was one of the few main-line expresses to stop at this station. Now most trains stop there.

In the second picture, taken on 8 September 1990, it would seem that a minor miracle has taken place. The platforms have been refurbished, two smart waiting shelters have been provided for passengers, and the station footbridge has been moved to a far more convenient position. To complete the scene, No 50049 *Defiance* is seen passing through the station with the 08.11 Exeter-Waterloo train.

These two pictures also provide an interesting comparison of livery styles. No 50019 is in the original BR livery and No 50049 in that of Network SouthEast; despite still being in the original livery, the former's headlight denotes that it had been refurbished at Doncaster Works, the first six locomotives to do so having been turned out in the original livery, and then repainted in the 'large logo' BR livery at a later date. *Both John Vaughan*

58 A splendid view of the Wiltshire countryside to the east of Salisbury, taken from the top of Fisherton tunnel. No 50005 *Collingwood* approaches Tunnel Junction with the 09.10 Waterloo-Exeter train on 14 April 1983.

The line to Southampton is off to the right of the picture, and in the middle background is the line which connects it to the Exeter line, also forming a convenient tri-angle for turning locomotives; this was much used when the steam specials ran from Salisbury to Yeovil Junction in the late 1980s. *Les Nixon*

59 A splendid scene at Salisbury Tunnel Junction on 18 August 1981 as No 50047 *Swiftsure*, in charge of the 07.37 train from Exeter to Waterloo, leaves Fisherton tunnel and takes the line to London, passing the LSWR signal box set between the Southampton and Waterloo lines. *Tom Heavyside*

60 On the evening of 12 August 1991 No 50046 *Ajax* coasts down grade from Fisherton tunnel with the 17.30 train from Waterloo to Yeovil Junction. Note the extreme curvature of the line, a feature of the eastern approach to the former LSWR station at Salisbury, and indeed the station itself. This was caused simply by the fact that the GWR arrived in Salisbury first, and the LSWR had to wind its line round the GWR station. *RS*

61 With Salisbury Cathedral overlooking the scene, No 50033 *Glorious* proceeds cautiously over the last few hundred yards to Salisbury station with the 16.15 from Waterloo to Yeovil Junction on 8 August 1991. The spire of the cathedral (which is currently undergoing restoration) is, at 400 feet, the highest mediaeval spire in Europe. The extensive goods sidings on the down side of the line are now disused, but those in the near foreground are in regular use. *RS*

62 Extreme wintry weather is generally not associated with southern England, but in January 1982 that was certainly not the case. In worsening conditions on 9 January, No 50045 *Achilles* has taken far longer than usual to travel from Waterloo to Salisbury with the 11.10 from London to Exeter. The formation is seen approaching Salisbury (past the old water tower) as the snow deepens. *John Vaughan*

63 The old GWR goods yard at Salisbury (which was situated at the north of the station) was used to berth exhibition coaches for many years, but was lifted in 1991. In clean 'large logo' livery, No 50036 *Victorious* is, unusually, parked on the ex-GWR metals on 25 September 1982. *John Vaughan*

64 There is plenty of Class 50 action at Salisbury on 5 May 1990 as No 50002 *Superb* (on the right) departs at 14.24 with the 12.28 train from Exeter St Davids to Waterloo. At platform 2 No 50029 *Renown* waits to depart with the 15.13 Salisbury to Waterloo, stopping at all stations to Basingstoke and then Woking and Clapham Junction, arriving at Waterloo at 16.48, having taken 105 minutes for the 83³/₄-mile journey. On the right-hand side of the picture is the former GWR station, which was closed in the 1930s. *RS*

65 Salisbury, 30 August 1990. No 50017 *Royal Oak* is reflected in one of the station's graceful Victorian windows, indicative of the style of the station. *RS*

SALISBURY TO EXETER

Salisbury lies in chalk downs that are littered with drovers' trails and prehistoric remains such as Stonehenge and Old Sarum, but which are now dedicated to tanks and artillery ranges. The cathedral was a renowned religious centre, and many will know the famous painting of it by Constable.

A mile from the station the lines divide near the ECC depot, the right-hand one being the GWR route to Westbury. These lines run side by side for a mile to Wilton Junction then part company. Our line now becomes single-track, with loops, as far as Templecombe. We run through the closed station which served Wilton, the one-time Saxon capital of Wessex, and continue 4 miles westwards to Dinton, which is also closed to passengers but serves a MoD goods spur to Chilmark. To the south we can see a long chalk escarpment overlooking Fovant village, into which are carved many regimental badges. From here the hills fold the line into many reverse curves.

At Tisbury, the next open station, there is a loop, recently opened to improve timings. Close by is a well-preserved mediaeval tithe barn, and a mile further on, near Hazeldon level crossing, is Wardour Castle, used recently for filming *Robin Hood*. The next station at Semley by the A350 is closed, but marks the summit on the Dorset border nearby, from which we descend the 1 in 100 towards Gillingham, 3 miles away. This market town is currently building a bypass which cuts across Station Road by the bridge over the River Stour.

We follow the river and climb the 1 in 100 to Buckhorn Weston tunnel which runs underneath Sandley Stud. From here we run 3 miles straight south-westwards, crossing the River Gale near Abbey Ford, and rising to Templecombe station. Much has been written about this famous junction with the Somerset & Dorset line - it is a gem of modern architecture and wins awards for the Best Kept Small Station (see the layout map on page 79).

We continue climbing, now on double tracks, through rich farmland to a summit between the nautically-named Milborne Wick and Milborne Port, and descend the 1 in 80 down the reverse curves of Sherborne bank. This affords a panoramic view of the two castles, old and new, that guard the outfall of Sherborne lake. This town had strategic importance from Roman to Mediaeval times, and now boasts of a famous public school.

Another 4 miles brings us to Yeovil Junction station, where a signal box and semaphores control the connection for the GWR lines from Westbury. The junction lies well south-east of the town, but is very important since the Town station closed. Our line now crosses into Somerset, then snakes round Sutton Bingham reservoir and undulates through wooded hills. A sharp 1 in 80 brings us into Crewkerne station, then a noisy start pulls us away at the same gradient through Crewkerne tunnel up to Hewish summit. After this we race down past Clapton Court and Forde Abbey and through Chard Junction (now closed) where a box controls a busy level crossing by a creamery.

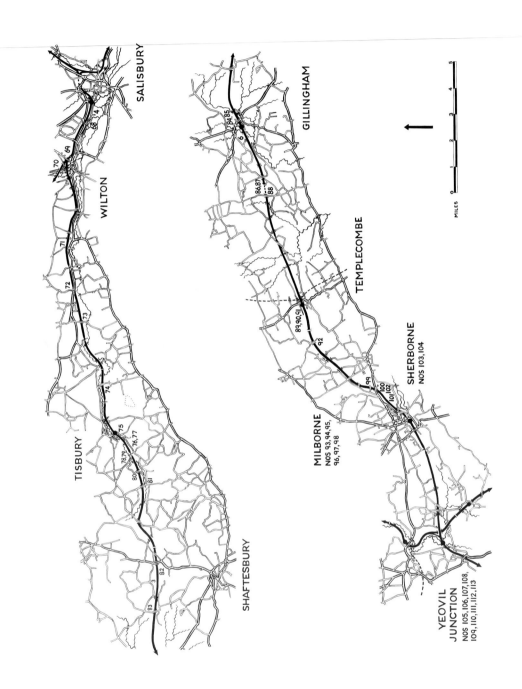

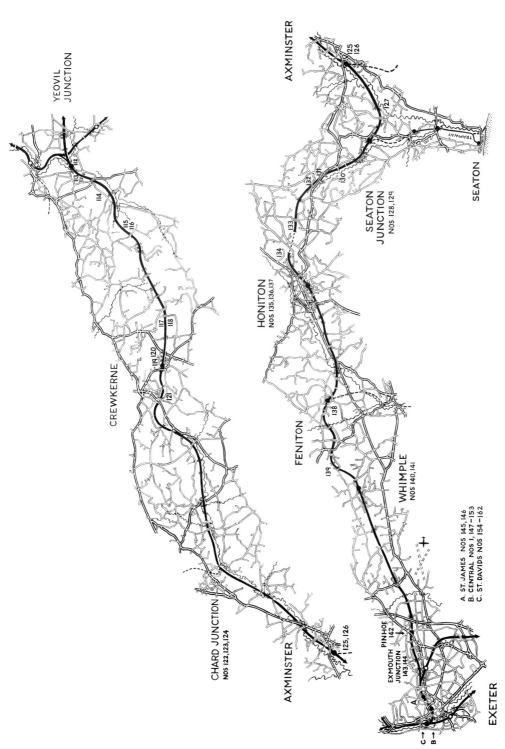

The route: Salisbury to Exeter (numbers refer to plates)

66 No 50046 *Ajax* poses beside the old LSWR signal box (now used as a store) at the western end of Salisbury's platform 3, on 8 August 1991. The locomotive has just brought in an ECS train from Eastleigh. After uncoupling from the train, the Class 50 will run round the stock, couple back onto the train, and depart at 15.13 for Waterloo. Note the sharp curvature of the platforms and canopies, a distinctive feature of Salisbury station. *RS*

67 Was this the last-ever occasion, following the withdrawal of No 50036, when a pair of old 'large logo'-liveried Class 50s double-headed a train? On 23 March 1991 a spare locomotive was required at Salisbury, so the 12.25 Exeter-Waterloo train was hauled by No 50046 *Ajax* and No 50031 *Hood*. The former was removed at Salisbury where this photograph was taken.

   The site of the Southern Railway locomotive shed at Salisbury (72B) was on the left-hand side of the line - in the area now overgrown with trees - and the shed yard was visible from the line. Right until the end of the steam on the region, the shed had a reputation for the cleanliness of its locomotives. In its heyday it had an allocation of around 60 locomotives, from 'Pacifics' to 0-6-0 tanks. *John Vaughan*

68 On an autumn morning, 2 October 1986, No 50015 *Valiant* leaves the city of Salisbury behind and heads west with the 09.10 Waterloo-Exeter train. In the misty background is Salisbury Cathedral, a prominent landmark in the area.

Note the small allotment on the lineside, a not untypical feature which started during the last war with the slogan 'Dig For Victory', when the Government urged people to use all available land for the growing of food. Alas, the author noted on a recent visit to this location (near the A36 road bridge) that the allotment is no more - a sign of the times! *RS*

We now speed south-westwards down into Devon to call at Axminster station. Just past this is the carpet factory that makes the town famous. Soon we turn north-west and start to climb at 1 in 100 - the foot of Honiton bank. We pass Seaton Junction station, now closed but which used to link with the seaside resort, and climb through the woods, now at 1 in 80, towards Honiton tunnel at the summit. Emerging from the tunnel, we have a panoramic view of Honiton, with its tall cream-coloured church tower just below the station.

The next station used to be called Sidmouth Junction, connecting to Sidmouth and Exmouth, but it was closed when the branch closed. It was, however, reopened for commuters and renamed Feniton. From here we run steadily down gradient through Devon farms, through Whimple with its cider factory, down to Broad Clyst (now closed) near Exeter Airport. We rise through Pinhoe station, also reopened, and Exmouth Junction past a great coal yard. After the short Blackboy tunnel we drop through St James Park Halt right under the stands of Exeter's football ground, and descend into Exeter Central station.

Central was originally a terminus (called Queen Street) until a link was cut through to the GWR station of Exeter St Davids. This involves the famous 1 in 37 bank and curve through St Davids tunnel which we descend carefully, meeting the GWR line from Plymouth at the western entrance to St Davids station, our journey's end.

69 Some 2 miles from Salisbury, the Exeter line and the former GWR route to Westbury split but run parallel for a few hundred yards until Wilton, where the Westbury line heads north-west. In this view taken on 26 July 1991, No D400 is seen heading the 17.30 Waterloo-Yeovil Junction train towards Wilton and the West Country. The line from Westbury is on the left-hand side, and forms part of the principal cross-country route from South Wales and Bristol to Southampton, Portsmouth and the South Coast. *RS*

70 Coming on to double track from single at the closed Wilton station on 12 July 1980 is No 50046 *Ajax* (still to be refurbished) with the 07.37 Exeter–Waterloo service. The old LSWR signal box was eventually demolished.

In steam days Wilton was famous as the locomotive change-over point for the all-Pullman 'Devon Belle' which ran to Ilfracombe and Plymouth. This luxury train (complete with Observation Car) was introduced in 1947 but was never a complete success, unlike the region's other Pullman services to Brighton, Bournemouth and Dover, and was withdrawn in 1954. *John Vaughan*

71 Crossing the pleasantly rural viaduct at Barford St Martin, west of Wilton, on 30 March 1991 is No 50018 *Resolution*, in charge of the 09.15 from the city of London to the cathedral city of Exeter. Originally double track to Exeter, the line was singled just west of Wilton station (see the previous picture) and, apart from a passing loop at Tisbury, is single as far as Templecombe. Looking at this scene, it is difficult to imagine that it was once double track. *John Vaughan*

72 *Sir Edward Elgar* was withdrawn in 1991, but on 7 April of that year No 50007 looks in 'fine fettle' as it powers the 15.30 Yeovil Junction-Waterloo train towards Salisbury and the capital. The location is Baverstock, midway between Barford St Martin and Dinton, in rural Wiltshire. Happily, the loco was subsequently reprieved. *RS*

73 Dinton station is now closed but at one time it was an important point on the route because of the large amount of military traffic. On 26 July 1991 No 50002 *Superb* hurries through the station with the 14.20 train from Exeter to Waterloo. The former up line is now a siding which provides a route to nearby military depots. The small LSWR building on the platform is interesting - it looks like a small signal box but Dinton's cabin was in fact situated on the down platform, so this must have been a workmen's hut or store. Note the military sidings on the left-hand side - both standard and narrow gauge. *RS*

74 In all-blue livery, and in pre-headlight days, No 50037 *Illustrious* has the power handle relaxed at Chicksgrove, a couple of miles east of Tisbury, with the 09.10 Waterloo-Exeter on 2 May 1981. *John Vaughan*

75 On 5 May 1990 No 50028 *Tiger* pulls away from Tisbury with the 11.15 Waterloo-Exeter train. The small Wiltshire town of Tisbury grew in size with the boom of the 1980s, and its importance on the Exeter route was increased when the Tisbury loop was opened to the east of the station in 1986. This loop, which provided accommodation for a 12-coach train, was a significant factor in the improvement of punctuality on the route. Tisbury also boasts one of the finest mediaeval tithe barns in the south of England. *RS*

76 and 77 These next two views show well the very pleasant countryside around the Tisbury area.

In the first picture, taken on 11 October 1986, No 50024 *Vanguard* is seen about half a mile west of Tisbury, as it powers the 13.10 from Waterloo towards Exeter.

The second view, taken at roughly the same location on 1 September 1990, shows No 50027 *Lion* with the 10.20 Exeter-Waterloo train, framed by an oak tree on the right and a Scots pine on the left. *Both RS*

78 Tisbury crossing, a mile west of Tisbury, now has electrically-controlled barriers, but at one time it had manual crossing gates (see below). On 1 September 1990 No 50029 *Renown* hurries past the crossing with the 09.15 (SO) Plymouth to Brighton train, via Salisbury and Southampton, due to arrive at Brighton at 16.03. This train also ran during the winter timetable of that year but was replaced in the summer of 1991 by the 09.25 (SO) service to Salisbury, Southampton and Waterloo, the first time for many years that Exeter did not have a Saturdays-only through service to the resort. *RS*

79 On 12 July 1980, when the delightful Tisbury crossing gates were manual, No 50014 *Warspite* hammers westwards with the 09.10 Waterloo-Exeter train. *John Vaughan*

80 D400, formerly No 50050 *Fearless*, was, along with Nos 50007 and 50031, one of the Class 50 'celebrity' locomotives used on the route, and is seen here at West Hatch near Semley on the afternoon of 10 April 1991 with the 13.15 Waterloo-Exeter train. *RS*

81 D400 once again, this time caught by the rays of the setting sun as it heads for London with the 14.55 Plymouth-Waterloo service on Sunday 7 April 1991.
    The location is near Wardour Castle, just west of Semley, which in recent times has found fame as the location for a *Robin Hood* film - a long way from Sherwood Forest! *RS*

82 Looking smart in the dark-blue Network SouthEast livery, No 50043 *Eagle* speeds along near Semley with the 17.15 from Waterloo on 5 May 1990. This train will arrive at Exeter St Davids at 20.37, having taken 3 hours 22 minutes for the 172½-mile journey. *RS*

83 Some 2 miles east of the Dorset town of Gillingham, we see No 50017 *Royal Oak* accelerating up the 1 in 114 with the 14.22 train from Exeter to Waterloo on 27 July 1991. Not to be confused with its Kentish namesake, the Dorset Gillingham is pronounced with a hard 'G'. Like Tisbury, its neighbour to the east, Gillingham has seen much expansion in recent years. *RS*

84 On 8 April 1991 the 12.28 Exeter to Waterloo train with D400 in charge draws into the smart-looking station of Gillingham. Although the station canopy is new, the station building dates back to the last century, with the steep pitch of the roof being a feature of Wessex architecture in Victorian days. This building provides a contrast with the more modern signal box on the left-hand side of the picture. In the background is a fertiliser warehouse and next to it a siding and freight facilities. *RS*

85 The 13.15 from Waterloo pauses at the down platform at Gillingham on Saturday 27 July 1991; in charge of the train is No 50046, the last Class 50 in the attractive 'large logo' livery. For convenience most trains use the down platform, except when the station is used as a passing loop. Once again a comparison of the station's different architectural styles can be made. The start of the siding which runs beside the warehouse can be seen just below the redundant buffer stops. *RS*

86 From Gillingham to the short tunnel at Buckhorn Weston, some 2 miles, it is a steep climb for down trains. Nearing the summit of that climb on Sunday 11 October 1986 is No 50045 *Achilles* in charge of the 09.10 Waterloo-Exeter train. Silver birch trees provide a fine backdrop. *RS*

87 On the same day as the previous picture, No 50049 *Defiance* (in 'large logo' livery before it was painted grey and renumbered as No 50149) leaves Buckhorn Weston tunnel and into the early autumn sunshine while in charge of the 09.40 from Exeter to London. This is the summit of the climb from Gillingham, so No 50049 will be able to coast down to the neat Dorset town which, amongst other things, is the possessor of a prize-winning Silver Band. Although the line is now single, it is quite easy to see that it was once double-track. *RS*

88 A panoramic view taken from the top of Buckhorn Weston tunnel on 31 July 1987. Climbing up to the tunnel from the Templecombe direction is an unidentified Class 50 with the 11.05 Exeter-Portsmouth train. *Les Nixon*

89   Templecombe was originally called Templecombe Junction. This most famous of West Country junctions, which connected the Waterloo-Exeter line with the late, and much lamented, Somerset & Dorset Joint Railway (SDJR) about which so much has been written, was obviously no longer a junction after the sad closure of the SDJR in March 1966. The accompanying plan shows the layout of the junction in its heyday.

Templecombe station itself closed a few weeks later in May 1966 and this picture, taken on 12 July 1980 before it was reopened, shows how derelict it had become, even though the platforms were still intact. Passing through the abandoned station is No 50027 *Lion* with the 13.10 Waterloo-Exeter train. *John Vaughan*

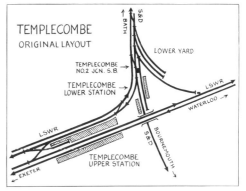

90   Happily, Templecombe station was reopened in 1982 and a new station building was completed in 1988 with, I might add, considerable support from the local community's railway action group.

Approaching the award-winning station (it now boasts the title 'Britain's Best Kept Small Station') on a frosty 19 February 1991 with the 08.11 up from Exeter St Davids is No 50049 *Defiance*. The number of cars in the car park gives some idea of the passenger traffic this small station now enjoys. *John Vaughan*

91   In this view of Templecombe, taken on 1 September 1990, we can see how the old footbridge has been restored, providing an easy link from the car park to the platform area. No 50003 *Temeraire* is about to stop at the station with the 06.52 Waterloo-Exeter train. Dominating the scene is the former Southern Railway signal box which also serves as a ticket office. Long after the station closed, this box was used to control the lengthy double-track section which starts a few yards west of the station. Note the hanging flower baskets, a feature of the station. *RS*

92 In the pleasant countryside at Stowell, south-west of Templecombe, No 50048 *Dauntless* heads for Sherborne with the 13.15 service from Waterloo to Exeter. For a mile out of Templecombe, down trains face a stiff climb of 1 in 100, but from then on, with one short exception, it is downgrade all the way to Yeovil Junction.

 The winding county boundary means that Templecombe and Yeovil are both in Somerset, but Sherborne, equidistant between the two, is in Dorset, as is Gillingham, situated to the east of Templecombe. *RS*

93 On 27 July 1991 No 50033 *Glorious* descends Sherborne bank with the 11.14 (SO) Southampton-Plymouth train which arrives at its destination at 15.50. *RS*

94 In steam days Sherborne bank was always a difficult task. Up trains faced a 4-mile climb with 2 miles at 1 in 80. On the evening of 8 April 1991 No 50037 *Illustrious* catches the last rays of the sun as it tops Sherborne bank in fine style with the 16.22 from Exeter St Davids to the capital. *RS*

95 A further seasonal contrast - high summer at Milborne Port, as No 50001 *Dreadnought* makes music in the hills as it accelerates the 11.50 Exeter-Waterloo train up the steep grade towards Templecombe on 15 July 1989. *John Vaughan*

96 On 15 August 1991 No 50033 *Glorious* speeds down Sherborne bank with the lightly-loaded 16.15 Waterloo to Yeovil Junction train. After reversing at Yeovil Junction, the locomotive will haul the empty stock back to Eastleigh, following in the path of the 17.38 Exeter St Davids to Waterloo train which departs from Yeovil Junction at 19.00. This was a weekday working only but it did provide Class 50, or 'Hoover', fans with a double bonus on Mondays to Fridays. At the rear of the train can be seen the three-arch bridge at Milborne Port. *RS*

97 No 50030 *Repulse* makes a fine sight in the late evening sunshine as it heads up Sherborne bank with the 16.22 Exeter-Waterloo train on 16 August 1991. Amongst many things, Class 50s are noted for the tremendous sound they make, especially, as on this occasion, when they are climbing a steep grade. The railways of the South West will never seem the same again without the sound of these formidable machines. *RS*

98 At the same spot on a glorious July evening in 1991 (the 27th), celebrity locomotive No D400 climbs Sherborne bank with the 16.22 Exeter to Waterloo train. The delightful countryside which abounds in this part of the world is well in evidence in this scene. In the background is the edge of Sherborne Park. *RS*

99 No 50017 *Royal Oak* coasts down Sherborne bank and approaches the hamlet of Oborne on 27 July 1991. The train is the Saturdays-only 09.15 Waterloo-Exeter service, arriving at Exeter St Davids at 12.36. On a Saturday this was the second down train from Waterloo, the first departing at 07.52, although for passengers from Basingstoke there was a down departure at 07.45, and from Salisbury a departure for Exeter at the early hour of 06.05. *RS*

100 On the same day No 50037 *Illustrious* climbs Sherborne bank at Oborne with the 10.20 Exeter-Waterloo train. Behind the hedge is the A30 between Salisbury to Yeovil; especially busy in summertime, it runs from London to Exeter and apart from a few places parallels the LSWR rail route. *RS*

101 Framed by a whitebeam tree, No 50030 *Repulse* starts the climb up Sherborne bank from the west with the 14.22 service from Exeter to the capital on 24 July, 1991. *RS*

102 No 50046 Ajax has just left Sherborne station and starts the climb up to Milborne Port with the 16.22 train from Exeter to Waterloo on 15 August 1991. In the background on the edge of Sherborne Park are the remains of Sherborne Old Castle, which was built in the 12th century. A newer castle resembling Blenheim Palace is situated on the south shore of the small lake which lies directly behind the Old Castle. Whereas the latter was built for the purpose of repelling attackers, the new Castle was built purely as a residence. RS

103 On 31 July 1987 Class 50 No 50042 *Triumph* calls at Sherborne station with an Exeter-Waterloo train. The pleasant market town of Sherborne has its origins in Roman times and boasts an attractive minster, making it popular with tourists. It is also the home of a famous public school. *Les Nixon*

104 At Sherborne (as at certain other stations on the route) down trains often use the up platform for all-round convenience. Business looks fairly brisk as No 50018 *Resolution* comes to a halt with the 15.15 from Waterloo on 8 April 1991.

 This picture gives a good view of the snowploughs attached to No 50018, one of only a few of the class to be fitted with them. *RS*

105 After leaving Sherborne the line runs through pleasant Dorset countryside to reach Yeovil Junction. This station is some 4 miles from Yeovil, a large market town which over the years has grown in prominence, being home to one of Europe's largest helicopter manufacturers.

Three-quarters of a mile east of Yeovil Junction, the old GWR line from Westbury to Weymouth runs under the LSWR line and there is a connecting spur from the GWR line to Yeovil Junction. This is known as the Yeovil Junction-Yeovil Pen Mill spur, Pen Mill being the name of the Western Region station in Yeovil itself. Passing the still surviving SR semaphore signals on the spur line, but itself running on the main line, No 50012 *Benbow* heads east with the 14.45 Yeovil Junction-Waterloo train on 5 April 1986, a day of permanent way engineering work. *John Vaughan*

Although obviously nowhere near as busy as in former days, Yeovil Junction can at times (by today's standards) show a reasonable amount of activity, as these next three pictures show.

106 In the first picture, taken on 5 April 1986, Class 33 No 33049 waits with the empty coaching stock of a terminated Brighton-Exeter train for the return working, whilst Class 50 No 50044 *Exeter* arrives with the diverted 08.15 Penzance-Paddington service. To complete the scene, No 50033 *Glorious* waits to depart with the 12.45 to Waterloo. *Gavin Morrison*

107 On 9 April 1991 Nos D400 and 50002 *Superb* depart from Yeovil Junction at 17.30 with the 16.22 Exeter-Waterloo train. *RS*

108 On the same day No 50001 *Dreadnought* waits to depart with the 14.22 Exeter-Waterloo train, whilst to complete the scene No 50007 *Sir Edward Elgar* approaches the station with the 13.15 service from Waterloo. To the left of the signal box is the commencement of the spur to the Western Region Weymouth line, and in front of it on the left the start of the line which leads to a small coal depot. RS

109 On the evening of 18 September 1987 No 50030 *Repulse* (then in 'large logo' livery) enters platform 1 at Yeovil Junction with the 16.18 from Exeter St Davids to Waterloo.

Originally the station had four platform faces (two island platforms), but now only the old up island platform is used, down trains using platform 2 of this. Also a Southern Railway footbridge at one time spanned the station but, as can be seen, it has been truncated. *RS*

110 An earlier scene at the Junction - 27 October 1980 - and although the second down island platform still retains its canopy, it has long been out of public use. The canopy has now long since gone, and the station buildings are used as offices, store rooms, etc. The train waiting to depart for Exeter is the 09.10 from Waterloo, with unrefurbished No 50021 *Rodney* in charge. Note the porters' trolleys stored under the footbridge. *Tom Heavyside*

111 No 50005 *Collingwood* stands at Yeovil Junction on 31 August 1990 with the 09.15 from Waterloo-Exeter, waiting to cross with the 10.20 from Exeter which will arrive behind No 50027 *Lion*. Although the line has been double-track from Templecombe, from Yeovil Junction, apart from short sections (notably at Chard Junction and Honiton stations), the line is now single until the outskirts of Exeter. *RS*

112 In steam days the Southern shed at Yeovil, with an allocation of around 20 locomotives, was based at the Town station, a joint station with the GWR on the latter's line from Westbury to Taunton. Town station, which was connected to Yeovil Junction by a spur line, was mainly served from the junction by an auto-train service, but main-line trains from Town also ran to Exeter, and in the Salisbury direction. Although Yeovil Junction had no shed, like many busy stations it had a turntable, which as can be seen it retains to this day. It was used by the steam locomotives which worked the steam specials from Salisbury in the late 1980s. On 5 May 1990 No 50002 *Superb* sets off from Yeovil with the 06.52 Waterloo– Exeter train. RS

113 Beneath a threatening sky No 50018 *Resolution* sets off from Yeovil Junction into the setting sun with the 17.05 service from Waterloo to Exeter on 30 August 1991. RS

114 On 27 July 1991 the 09.45 Exeter-Waterloo train with No 50037 *Illustrious* in charge is seen between East Coker and Barwick, about a mile west of Yeovil Junction, near the Yeovil-Dorchester road. We are now in Somerset again - although Yeovil is in Somerset, Yeovil Junction is just over the border in Dorset, the boundary being a few yards from the station. *RS*

115 and 116 Some 4 miles after leaving Yeovil Junction the line runs through some fine Somerset countryside, skirting natural woodlands which are home to rare birds such as buzzards. The three principal woods in the area are Coker Wood, Pen Wood and Chedington Woods. In the photograph on the left Class 50 No 50030 *Repulse* passes the edge of Coker Wood as it races westwards to Crewkerne with the 08.40 train from Waterloo to Exeter on 29 August 1991.

Taken on the same day the photograph above shows No 50017 *Royal Oak* heading eastwards with the 09.45 from Exeter to the capital. In the background Pen Wood covers the northern half of Birts Hill, which is 182 metres high and straddles the Somerset/Dorset border. *Both RS*

117 On 26 May 1991 Nos 50046 *Ajax* and 50003 *Temeraire* provide superpower - 32 cylinders and 5,400 bhp - for the 12.55 Waterloo-Exeter train. The location is North Perrott, some 2 miles east of Crewkerne. RS

118 Celebrity locomotive No D400 is caught by the camera as it accelerates the 14.28 Exeter-Waterloo train out of Crewkerne near North Perrott on 26 May 1991. RS

119 No 50030 *Repulse* approaches Crewkerne with the 12.40 from Waterloo and passes the old goods shed, now used by a local coal supplier. The modern-looking signal box is now used as a tool store, and just off the right-hand side of the picture (where there were once sidings) there is now a small coal depot, but not connected to the line. *RS*

120 Crewkerne can still boast a fine-looking station complete with stationmaster's house, all of which has recently been refurbished. The modern-looking canopy is the only major recent addition, which contrasts sharply with the beautiful gables of the Victorian building, whose date - 1859 - is inscribed in the stonework of the small gable just above the locomotive. The train, hauled by No 50017, is the 14.28 from Exeter to Waterloo, and the date for this and the previous picture is 28 July 1991. *RS*

121 On leaving Crewkerne station, westbound trains face a short but steep climb of 1 in 80 up to Hewish summit, passing through the short Crewkerne tunnel. In fact, this steep gradient starts about half a mile east of the station, so that the Class 50s can be guaranteed to make a noisy start with down trains. On 5 April 1986 No 50025 *Invincible* approaches Crewkerne tunnel with the diverted 13.05 from Paddington to Penzance. *Gavin Morrison*

122   Chard Junction is our next location as No 50022 *Anson* hurries over the level crossing with the 11.10 Waterloo-Exeter train on 4 May 1982. Guarding the crossing is a fine LSWR signal box, which has now been replaced (see opposite).

The Great Western branch line from Creech Junction, east of Taunton on the main line to Paddington, ran in to Chard Junction station, but this branch line was closed in 1962, and Chard Junction station itself was closed in 1966, although a lengthy passing loop was retained. *Tom Heavyside*

123   Passing the old goods shed at Chard Junction on 28 July 1991 is No 50033 *Glorious* in charge of the 11.05 from Exeter to Waterloo. Just off the left of the picture is sited a very large dairy, which in the past created a lot of rail traffic. *RS*

124 The new signal box at Chard Junction guards the busy crossing over which most of the milk tankers from the dairy cross to gain access to the A30 road, which is situated some 3 miles to the north. *RS*

125 No 50009 *Conqueror* leaves the small Devon market town of Axminster behind as it heads eastwards for London with the 14.20 from Exeter St Davids on 4 May 1982. *Tom Heavyside*

126 On 28 May 1985 the 14.20 from Exeter to Waterloo arrives at Axminster station with No 50046 in charge. Looking at this scene it is hard to imagine that Axminster was once a busy junction station, with the branch line to Lyme Regis starting from a bay platform on the right-hand side of the picture. The line headed away south-westwards out of the station, crossed the main line by means of a flyover, and headed south and then due east to the resort of Lyme Regis, some 6¾ miles from Axminster. From the 1920s until 1961 the branch was famous for its steam motive power - the 4-4-2 tank engines designed by Adams for the LSWR, which it seemed were ideally suited to the sharp curvatures and gradients of the line. The branch was closed in 1965. Axminster itself is famous for its carpets - note the factory above the rear of the train. *RS*

127 No 50040 *Centurion* with the 09.10 Waterloo-Exeter train is caught by the camera near Whitford, some 2 miles west of Axminster on 1 August 1987. *Les Nixon*

128 Only the up platform and buildings now remain of Seaton Junction. As with Axminster, it is hard to imagine how much has now gone. There were four tracks through the station, plus a small goods yard at the west end on the up side, which catered for the adjacent Express Dairies depot. The Seaton branch platform was off the left-hand side of the picture opposite the station building. The branch line and Seaton Junction station were both closed in March 1966. Speeding through what remains of the station on the evening of 25 May 1991 is No D400 with the 17.42 from Exeter to London. RS

129 Approaching Seaton Junction from the west on 3 April 1988 is No 50008 *Thunderer* with the 14.20 service from Exeter to Waterloo. At this date there were still a couple of sidings left, but these have now been taken up.

A mile to the east of Seaton Junction is the start of Honiton bank, some 7 miles in length with gradients as steep as 1 in 70 for down trains. *RS*

130 A pleasant reminder of pre-Grouping days, found on a farm occupation bridge near Wilmington. *RS*

131 No 50029 *Renown* climbs Honiton bank near Wilmington with the 06.15 Salisbury-Exeter train on 16 August 1991. At this location the line parallels the A35 road through this lovely Devon valley. *RS*

132 Glowing in the gloomy evening light is No 50031 *Hood* as it approaches Wilmington road bridge with the 17.15 from Waterloo on 25 May 1991. The locomotive had just been beautifully painted by the staff of Laira depot to commemorate the 50th anniversary of the sad event of the sinking of the naval vessel of the same name. *RS*

133 No 50001 *Dreadnought* is within a mile of the summit of Honiton bank as it heads westwards on a crisp 19 February 1985 with the 09.10 from Waterloo. *RS*

134 At the summit of Honiton bank is the western end of Honiton tunnel. On 28 March 1981 No 50016 *Barham*, in all-blue livery, has just left the tunnel and picks up speed on the down grade with the 14.20 from Exeter to Waterloo. The gradient through the tunnel is 1 in 132, which in steam days would make for unpleasant conditions for the footplate crew. *John Vaughan*

135 For modern traction fans there is arguably no better sight than a pair of Class 50s in action, both visually and aurally. This was certainly the case on 22 July 1990 as Nos 50005 *Collingwood* and 50027 *Lion* make a spirited and no doubt noisy start up the steep gradient out of Honiton with the Sundays 17.22 Exeter-Waterloo train. *Michael J.Collins*

136 The station in the small but busy market town of Honiton, famous for lace-making, is set on the hillside above the main town. Running into the station on 1 August 1987 is No 50030 *Repulse* with the 13.10 from Waterloo. Although all trains now stop at Honiton, this was not always the case. In the past it was mainly served by local trains with very few expresses stopping there. *Les Nixon*

137 On Sunday 28 July 1991 the 08.15 Waterloo-Exeter train pulls out of Honiton with No 50017 *Royal Oak* in charge. The Southern Railway-style signal box is still in use to control the double track through the station, but nowadays both up and down trains as a rule use the down platform. *RS*

138   Sidmouth Junction station was closed in 1967, but due to the growth in population in the area it was reopened in 1971 under its original name of Feniton. On 25 April 1987 No 50041 *Bulwark* pulls away from the station with the 12.35 from Exeter.

    The line to Sidmouth ran from the station area off to the left of the picture; at Tipton St Johns the line forked, and a second line carried on to Budleigh Salterton and Exmouth, allowing through workings to these Devon holiday resorts *via* Sidmouth Junction. *Michael J.Collins*

139 No 50029 *Renown* accelerates the 08.26 Basingstoke-Exeter train away from the curves at Newtown, some 2 miles west of Feniton on 3 April 1988. *RS*

140 On 27 March 1988 No 50020 *Revenge* leaves the picturesque village of Whimple behind as it heads for London with the 14.20 from Exeter St Davids. At the time the up main line was being used as a siding and as access to the small goods yard (hence the wrong-line working), but all this has now been lifted. *RS*

141 Although this picture was taken in 1988, Whimple still retains a lot from its Southern Railway days. The old goods shed still looks in reasonable order, although by this time it was probably out of use altogether. The sidings leading to it, which also served the adjacent Whiteways Cider factory, have gone but there is still a siding alongside the shed leading to the goods platform; the up main line is used as an access siding. Also worthy of note is the SR concrete telegraph pole which doubles as a lamp-post.

Entering the station on 27 March 1988 is No 50023 *Howe* with the 11.10 from Waterloo, bound for Exeter St Davids. *RS*

142 With grey-and-blue Mark I coaches infiltrating a Mark 2b set, No 50014 *Warspite* passes what, on 18 April 1981, were the abandoned platforms of Pinhoe, with the 16.20 Exeter-Waterloo train. The station was closed in 1966 but happily was reopened in May 1983 although, to a lesser extent like Whimple and Feniton, not all trains stop here. The line is single from Yeovil Junction (with passing loops) but from Pinhoe westwards to Exeter it is double track. *John Vaughan*

143 On 16 September 1990 No 50009 *Conqueror* speeds downgrade at Exmouth Junction with the 10.40 from Waterloo. The line to Exmouth veers off to the right at the rear of the train.

Exmouth Junction locomotive shed (72A) was situated roughly at the rear of the coal wagons in the yard. This shed was one of the Southern Railway's largest, with an allocation of around 100 locomotives, from diminutive tank engines to the mighty Bulleid 'Merchant Navy' 'Pacifics'. The extensive coal yard still sees a fair amount of activity. *Gavin Morrison*

144 The 13.33 from Exeter St Davids to Waterloo, with No 50047 *Swiftsure* in charge, leaves Blackboy tunnel and climbs the 1 in 100 up to Exmouth Junction on 10 August 1985. *Gavin Morrison*

145 No 50002 *Superb* threads the deep cutting at the western end of Blackboy tunnel and approaches St James Park Halt with the 08.40 from Waterloo. *RS*

146 The home of Exeter City Football Club is St James Park and nearby is St James Park Halt. On 28 April 1982 No 50050 *Fearless* climbs through the halt with the 14.20 from Exeter St Davids to Waterloo. Note the allotments, a characteristic feature of 'spare' railway land. *Tom Heavyside*

147 No 50038 *Formidable* approaches Exeter Central station with the 09.10 service from Waterloo on 1 May 1984. Overlooking the scene is a fine example of a Southern Railway rail-built three-doll bracket signal. *Hugh Ballantyne*

148 Turning round to face in the other direction, we see No 50005 *Collingwood* departing from Exeter Central station with the 09.45 from Exeter St Davids to Waterloo on 27 May 1984.

At this date, Exeter Central box was still in use and the Exeter area was still using semaphore signalling, but this was shortly to change when the new power box at Exeter St Davids came into operation early in the following year. RS

149 No 50007 *Sir Edward Elgar* approaches Central station on 3 May 1991 with the 11.15 from Waterloo. The old Southern Railway signal box is now obviously out of use, but still being used as a tool store.

  The land to the right of the picture is now a car park but was originally carriage sidings and a coal depot. As can be seen, several of the main running lines have been taken up, and at one time the up platform extended almost to the signal box. The lines on either side of the box run to a small goods yard which sees infrequent use. *RS*

150 On a cloudy but pleasant spring day, 2 April 1988, No 50010 *Monarch* eases into platform 2 at Exeter Central with the 13.10 from Waterloo. The bay platform on the right (platform 1) is mainly used for shuttle services to St James Park Halt.

  The former Southern Railway-style concrete footbridge straddles the up and down platforms and connects to the North Road entrance to the station. The main entrance to the station is in Queen Street, this being the name of the original LSWR station on this site. The new Southern station known as Exeter Central was opened in 1933. *RS*

151 Looking a glorious sight after a fine repaint by Laira (see plate 132), No 50031 *Hood* pauses at Exeter Central on its 'maiden voyage' with the 09.25 from Plymouth to Waterloo via Southampton. As can be seen, there were originally four roads through the station. The small goods yard on the right is also a reminder of more prosperous days. RS

152 On 30 July 1983 No 50008 *Thunderer* tops the 1 in 37 climb up from Exeter St Davids station and approaches platform 3 of Central station with the 11.40 St Davids to Waterloo train. *RS*

153 No 50049 *Defiance* leaves the short St Davids tunnel behind and climbs the last few yards of the 1 in 37 up to Exeter Central station with the 09.45 Exeter-Waterloo on 3 May 1991.

The area off the left of the picture, which is now a BR store yard and car park, was home to carriage sidings and small coal and timber depots. Locomotives would also stand here whilst waiting to take out various portions of expresses such as the 'Atlantic Coast Express', for it was at Central station that the trains were divided for North Cornwall and North Devon, etc. *RS*

154 The splendid GWR signal box at the west end of Exeter St Davids overlooks No 50011 *Centurion* as it eases round the sharp curve at the bottom of the 1 in 37 from Central station and approaches St Davids station with the 06.50 from Waterloo on 27 July 1984. The main lines to Newton Abbot and Plymouth run in front of the signal box. *RS*

155 A view through the impressive gantry that used to stand at the west end of St Davids station, as No 50012 *Benbow* approaches platform 4 with the 09.20 Sundays Salisbury to Exeter service on 13 May 1984. The locomotive is crossing the former GWR line to South Devon and Plymouth. *Hugh Ballantyne*

156 On the afternoon of 11 April 1983 No 50033 *Glorious* pulls out of the west end of platform 4 at St Davids with the ECS of a Waterloo train. After pulling forward and clearing the station, it will then reverse the stock into the sidings on the up side of the station. More recently, the empty stock of Waterloo trains was stabled at the northern end of the station area. *RS*

157 No 50046 *Ajax* waits to leave Exeter St Davids with the 17.42 to Waterloo on 31 August 1991. *RS*

158 On 1 September 1990 the afternoon sun highlights No 50017 *Royal Oak* as it pulls out of the old GWR St Davids station with the 16.22 to Waterloo. Note the fine station buildings, the result of a rebuilding of 1911-14. *RS*

159 and 160 These two pictures taken on 26 May 1984 show the site of the former GWR locomotive shed at Exeter St Davids (83C), which became a refuelling depot for diesel locomotives and, at the time that these pictures were taken, a stabling point for empty coaching stock.

In the above scene No 50027 *Lion* is moving out of the sidings with the ECS for the 16.18 to Waterloo, passing a GWR semaphore signal with route indicator. In the centre background of the picture No 50002 *Superb* stands by the refuelling bay, while stabled on the left is No 50042 *Triumph*, behind which are Class 45 No 45129 and Class 47 47603. The scene below features a broadside of No 50042 and the front end of No 50027. *Both RS*

161 We finish our journey from Waterloo to Exeter appropriately with two nocturnal scenes, taken at Exeter St Davids station on the evening of 30 October 1984. The first scene shows No 50019 *Ramillies* waiting to leave platform 3 with the 17.33 to Waterloo. RS

162 Our final picture shows, on the left, No 50010 *Monarch* on the 19.34 to Waterloo, whilst on the right No 50004 *St Vincent* stands with an ECS train. RS

INDEX

(Numbers refer to pages, not plates)

Locomotives
50001   81, 91, 108
50002   30, 46, 57, 67, 90, 94,
        116, 125
50003   79, 98
50004   46, 47, 127
50005   53, 93, 110, 118
50007   19, 47, 50, 66, 91, 119
50008   45, 107, 121
50009   103, 115
50010   119, 127
50011   122
50012   89, 122
50013   14, 36
50014   70, 115
50015   23, 63
50016   109
50017   39, 42, 48, 51, 58, 73,
        84, 97, 100, 111, 124
50018   32, 33, 36, 65, 88, 95
50019   52, 126
50020   113
50021   93
50022   28, 102
50023   29, 114
50024   68
50025   29, 101
50027   22, 30, 34, 44, 69, 78,
        110, 125
50028   26, 68
50029   40, 57, 70, 107, 113
50030   83, 86, 92, 96, 100,
        111
50031   35, 40, 62, 108, 120
50033   32, 51, 55, 80, 82, 90,
        102, 123
50036   56
50037   37, 44, 67, 81, 85, 96
50038   117
50039   23
50040   31, 104
50041   21, 112
50042   88, 125
50043   20, 73
50044   25, 27, 90

50045   27, 56, 75
50046   41, 49, 55, 62, 65, 74,
        87, 98, 104, 123
50047   54, 116
50048   18, 19, 25, 43, 48, 80
50049   35, 52, 76, 78, 121
50050 (D400) 2, 38, 64, 71, 72, 74,
        84, 90, 99, 105, 117

Locations
Andover   51
Axminster   103

Barford St Martin   65
Basing   11, 43
Basingstoke   44
Battledown flyover   46-7
Baverstock   66
Brookwood   38
Buckhorn Weston   75-7

Chard Junction   102-3
Chicksgrove   67
Clapham Junction   24-7
Coker Wood   96-7
Crewkerne   102-3

Dinton   67

Earlsfield   27
East Coker   96
Esher   32
Exeter Central   2, 117-21
   St Davids   122-7
   St James   116-7
Exmouth Junction   115-6

Farnborough   40
Feniton (Sidmouth Junction)   112

Gillingham   11, 73-4
Grately   52

Hersham   32
Honiton   110-1

Honiton bank   108-9
Hook   42
Hurstbourne   50-1
Milborne Port (Sherborne bank)
   81-4

New Malden   29
Newtown   113
Nine Elms   23
North Perrott   98-9

Oborne (Sherborne bank)   84-5
Overton   48

Pinhoe   115
Pirbright Junction   39-40

Raynes Park   29

St Denys   14
Salisbury   9, 53-8, 62-3
Seaton Junction   105-6
Semley   3, 72-3
Sherborne   86-7
Sidmouth Junction (Feniton)   112
Stowell   80
Surbiton   30-1

Templecombe   78-9
Tisbury   68-71

Vauxhall   22

Walton on Thames   33
Waterloo   6, 18-21
West Hatch   71
Weybridge   34-5
Whimple   113-4
Whitchurch   48-9
Wilmington   107-8
Wilton   64-5
Wimbledon   28
Winchfield   41
Woking   36
Worting Junction   45-6

Yeovil Junction   89-95